50 years

PRESENTED BY

CHRISTOPHER N. UFERE

IN HONOR OF

HIS GRANDPARENTS

MR. & MRS. OKORE OGBONNA
AND

MR. & MRS. THOMAS A. UFERE

2002

WESTMINSTER SCHOOLS   SMYTHE GAMBRELL LIBRARY

In memory of my grandmother

Published in the United States in 2001 by The Millbrook Press, Inc.
2 Old New Milford Road, Brookfield, Connecticut 06804

First published in Great Britain in 2001 by Frances Lincoln Limited
4 Torriano Mews, Torriano Avenue, London NW5 2RZ

Edited, designed, and produced by Frances Lincoln Limited

Saying Good-bye © 2001 by Frances Lincoln Limited
Text and illustrations © 2001 by Ifeoma Onyefulu

Library of Congress Cataloging–in–Publication Data
Onyefulu, Ifeoma.
Saying goodbye : a special farewell to Mama Nkwelle / Ifeoma Onyefulu.
p.   cm.
ISBN 0-7613-1965-4 (lib. bdg.)
1. Funeral rites and ceremonies—Nigeria—Juvenile literature. 2. Nigeria—Social life and customs—Juvenile literature.
[1. Funeral rites and ceremonies—Nigeria. 2. Nigeria—Social life and customs.] I. Title.

GT3289.N6 O59 2001
393'.9—dc21 00-030540

Set in Angie

Printed in Singapore

1 3 5 7 9 8 6 4 2

Saying Good-bye

A Special Farewell to Mama Nkwelle

Ifeoma Onyefulu

The Millbrook Press
Brookfield, Connecticut

–Author's Note

As a teenager, I was often embarrassed to see my grandmother, Mrs. Agnes Uso Ikwensi, getting up to glide and float like a butterfly in front of everyone. She was always dancing. It was only later that I learned she had once been a professional dancer.

To many in Nkwelle Ezunaka, in eastern Nigeria, my grandmother was the greatest traditional dancer of her generation. People say that every time she danced, she was lifted up afterward and carried shoulder-high back to the house of her father, Chief Ikelinwu Asali.

At her funeral, I asked my great-uncle Chike why she was carried like this. He replied, "Because no one wanted her feet to touch the ground again!" Then he added, "And because everyone wanted to see the great dancer."

But to me, she was just my grandmother — wise and intelligent, always full of advice. To my son Ikenna, the narrator of this book, she was warm and caring. She was also a grandmother to many other children in the village, looking after them during the day while their parents were out working.

I am proud to be able to tell my own children that I have had the privilege of seeing my grandmother dance — even though, at the time I saw her, old age might have slowed her down a little!

My great-grandmother gave me some *akwu* (palm kernels). Now that she has died I am going to grow them.

I remember my great-grandmother very well, especially her face—her lovely eyes, nose, and mouth. When I went to see her, she always said, "Welcome, Ikenna. You are as bright and beautiful as the sun."

Do you know what I used to call her? I called her Mama Nkwelle, because she was nice, and everybody in Nkwelle village thought so, too.

When Mama Nkwelle died, everyone came to say good-bye. Uncle Asika said it was a special good-bye. It took more days that I can count on my fingers. No wonder everybody worked so hard getting ready for it!

My friends Uzo and Maria made special white clothes for me, my grandmother, my mother, and my uncles and aunts to wear.

Then some of my cousins helped with the cleaning and sweeping of the grounds of Mama Nkwelle's home. Other cousins arranged chairs for people to sit on.

My aunts prepared a rice meal for the *Umuada* — Mama Nkwelle's nieces and cousins. They had walked all the way from Amuche, where my great-grandmother was born, to be with us for the celebrations.

My uncles set up canopies to shelter guests from the sun.

The night before the big day, my cousins, uncles, aunts, grandmother, and the Umuada gathered and stayed up all night—we call it holding a wake. They sang songs and danced for Mama Nkwelle at her home.

The next day was special, because it was the first time people said their good-byes to Mama Nkwelle. There were lots of loud bangs, one after the other. They were so loud, they shook the ground and nearly squashed my ears. Uncle Asika said it was a twenty-one gun salute. He said the guns were fired to say the celebration was about to begin, and to show respect for Mama Nkwelle's long life.

I wore my new white clothes, and did some drawings of my great-grandmother on the ground to remind people of her.

When I went into Mama Nkwelle's house, the Umuada were sitting around a decorated bed which had once been Mama Nkwelle's—to be close to her, they said. Everyone went in to see Mama Nkwelle's picture and to say how sorry they were.

We were there a long time. Then a priest from Mama Nkwelle's church said prayers beside her grave. He also blessed a bowl of kola nuts, and my uncles offered them to the guests.

Soon I heard the sound of drums. They were nice and loud. People began to dance.

My grandmother, the daughter of Mama Nkwelle, was asked to dance. Then my great-uncles, the sons of Mama Nkwelle, took their turn at dancing. Everyone gave gifts—cows, chickens, money, and soft drinks—and there was more singing and dancing.

Then we watched the *Nwadiana*—in-laws—giving special gifts of cloth called *Ikpuawa* to my grandmother and her brothers. When I asked Uncle Asika what "in-laws" are, he said that my grandfather, my father, and my aunties' husbands are my in-laws.

Soon it was my grandfather's turn to present his gift. My grandmother walked beside him as he presented the cloth to the rest of Mama Nkwelle's family.

Suddenly, everyone was asking for me. "Why?" I asked my grandfather. He said that because my father could not come to the celebration, my big brother and I were to take his place. So we were in-laws, too! One of my uncles and my grandfather showed us what to do.

My brother walked up to the table carrying his cloth over one arm, while I walked slowly in front. Here are some of the cloths that were given to the family.

My grandmother and great uncles said thank you to everyone by giving them bowls and cups with Mama Nkwelle's picture on them.

Later, my grandmother was asked to hold the picture of her mother, Mama Nkwelle, while she danced. Uncle Asika said that is what people do when someone dies.

But the biggest dance of all was on the fourth day, when people from the village of Amuche came along and joined in. They were so sad that Mama Nkwelle had died, they all called out "Uso! Uso!" (her first name) as they ran into her sitting room.

After that, some of the people went home.

MRS AGNES USO EKWENE

There were four days when nothing happened. Then one day, I heard four loud bangs. Uncle Asika said it was a four-gun salute, to remind everyone to come to Mama Nkwelle's house just for the day. This time there was no drumming or singing and dancing, because it was a quiet time to remember Mama Nkwelle.

And Uncle Asika was right. Everywhere was as quiet as a stone, except when people were talking to each other.

My great-aunt said to me, "Do you remember what your great-grandmother used to say to you?"

And I said, "Eyes, ears, and nose," because Mama Nkwelle always said that when it was time to go home.

My great-aunt laughed. "Child, you are so like your great-grandmother. She was one for remembering things. And why did she say that?"

"Because eyes, ears, and a nose will help me to learn things every day," I said.

Uncle Asika said there would be another seven-gun salute in twelve days' time, but today we would go on being quiet. He was right again, because there was no noise apart from the humming sound everyone made as they told each other stories.

My great-aunt said to me, "Ikenna, your great-grandmother used to dance like a butterfly, the most beautiful butterfly in the world, when she was a young girl. She won lots of prizes, too! People would lift her up on their shoulders after she had danced. They loved her because she made them happy."

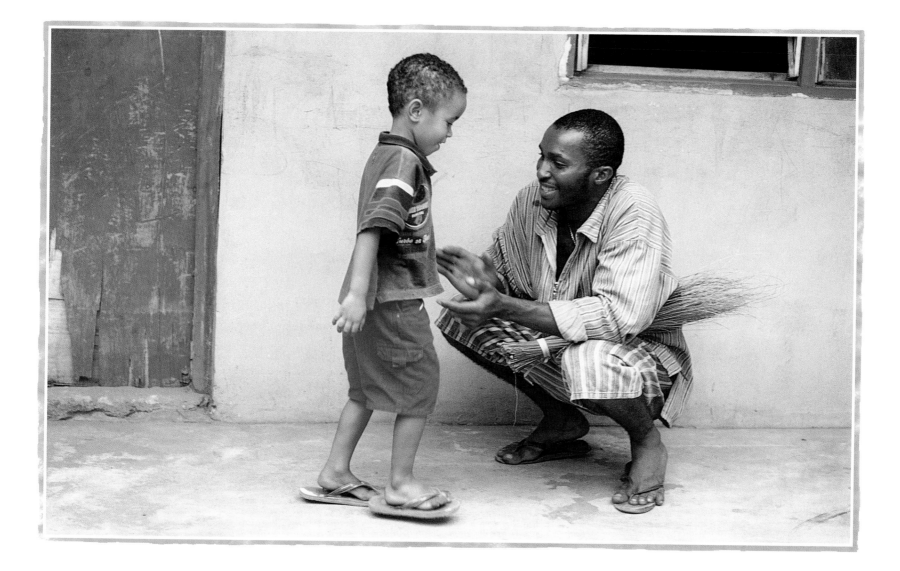

"I wish I was a dancer!" I said. Uncle Patrick said I could be. So he clapped for me and I danced a bit — but not like a butterfly.

The next day, I showed Uncle Patrick my special present from Mama Nkwelle, and he said that the kernels would grow into palm trees. So I took my hoe, went into the garden, chose a nice place—one Mama Nkwelle would have liked—and dug some little holes. Then I planted the *akwu* kernels.

"My palm trees!" I said. "When I come and look at them, I will think of Mama Nkwelle. She will be right in the middle of them, looking after me! I know she will."